Fishbone

❧ Fishbone

poems by Aimee Nezhukumatathil

Snail's Pace Press, Inc.
Cambridge, NY

The Snail's Pace Press, Inc.
85 Darwin Road
Cambridge, New York 12816

Darby Penney, Publisher
Ken Denberg, Editor
Naton Leslie, Associate Editor
Stuart Bartow, Associate Editor

The Snail's Pace Press, Inc. is a member of the Council of Literary
Magazines and Presses (CLMP).

Special thanks to Siena College and its Greyfriar Living Literature Series

Cover: "Fishbone," acrylic on canvas panel, by Aimee Nezhukumatathil
Back cover photo: Michael Lohre
Cover design: Darby Penney

ISBN 0-9575273-2-5

ACKNOWLEDGMENTS

Ooty Lake, Wrap *Beloit Poetry Journal*

Speak, Arachne, One Bite *Chelsea*

Our Time *Chiron Review*

Cocoa Beach, Off-Season *Green Hills Literary Lantern*

Peacocks, Winter Games *The Massachusetts Review*

Spices *Nimrod: International Journal of Poetry and Fiction*

Wedding Sheets *Puerto del Sol*

Sara, Embarrassed *The Rio Grande Review*

Stealing Song, Firsts *The Spoon River Poetry Review*

What I Learned From the Incredible Hulk aapeared in *The Mid-American Review* in a slightly different version

Fishbone, Ooty Lake (reprinted), One Bite (reprinted) from Babaylan: An Anthology of Filipina and Filipina-American *Poetry and Art,* Nick Carbo and Eileen Tabios, eds., Aunt Lute Press

Speak (reprinted) from *The Beacon Best of 2000: Great Writing by Women and Men of All Colors and Cultures*, Edwidge Danticat, ed., Beacon Press

Mouth Stories received first place in the 1999 *Atlantic Monthly's* Emerging Writer Competition

Special thanks to the following for their suport: my colleagues at the Ohio State University's Creative Writing Program, especially David Citino; Sara Sutherland, Americ Quandt, Ron Degenfelder, Sharon Wong, Eileen Tabos and Nick Carbo, OSU's Critical Difference Grants, Jesse Lee Kerchevel and the Wisconsin University Institute for Creative Writing, Michael Lohre, JoAnn, and my parents, Mathew and Paz.

- A.N.

TABLE OF CONTENTS

FISHBONE

At dinner, my mother says if one gets stuck
in your throat, roll some rice into a ball
and swallow it whole. She says things
like this and the next thing out of her mouth

is *did you know Madonna is pregnant?*
But I want to ponder the basket of fried smelt
on the table, lined with paper towels to catch
the grease—want to study their eyes

like flat soda, wonder how I'm supposed
to eat them whole. Wonder why we can't
have normal food for breakfast like at Sara's house—
Cheerios, or sometimes if her mother is home:

buttered toast and soft-boiled eggs
in her grandmother's dainty blue egg cups
and matching blue spoon. Safe. Pretty.
Nothing with eyes. Under the flakes of fried crust,

I see a shimmer of skin as silver as foil,
like the dimes my mother tapes to a board
for each year I'm alive. How she tucked this
into my suitcase before I left for college

and I forgot about '93 *and* '95. How she said
she'll never find a '93, and shouldn't this
be a great thing to one day put into an oak frame,
but not now, not until we find the missing coin?

How we don't have many traditions left, thanks
to Your Father. These are the things she says
instead of a blessing to our food. These are the words
that stick inside me as I snap off the next head.

STEALING SONG

"WELCOME TO THE PHILIPPINES, THE ONLY CATHOLIC
COUNTRY IN ASIA! (beware of pickpockets)"
                                    - *billboard outside Metro Manila*

We dupe you kindly:
        an extra letter silk-screened
on stacks of T-shirts
in the *Los Santos* markets.
        Or maybe in a fliver
of colored bills, a wave of hand
as we rush you through
        the checkout line, sliding some
under the counter for later.
But we smile.
        We smile always, talk clicks
and questions about the latest
American movie star, offer tips
        on where to dine. I pray
you don't see my hand
in your shopping bag, tucking
        that scarf for your sister—blue
as lobster blood—into my pocket.
The thrill of your bauble
        in my palm is almost
like having pesos to buy it
myself. We mean no harm.
        We will never split
your skin, not like ones
from the North. We sing
        your safe travel, bags
a little lighter than before.
We wish you dreams
        of sweet tomato and platters
of pig heads, mouths open,
saying *ah* and *oh*.

2

WEDDING SHEETS

So what shall she tell the townsfolk, the priests,
her mother?
The wedding sheets rest rumpled:
gold threads and crisp rosettes
embroider the edges. When the bedding
hangs outside her new husband's window
· for the Elders to cluck about
over honeyed bread and warm milk,
there will be no sacred stains to show.

Years before, just once,
she sighed in the coastal clearing
of a sugarcane field, gave in to Ocean's warmth
between her legs and his whispered promises
that the other village boys would never know,
that she could soon join him in a country
so cold, mango trees could never thrive.

While her husband washes
his body of the gardenia
blossoms tucked in her hair,
she slips into the back room,
grasps the blade until her knuckles
blanch—almost glow—dots
the wedding sheets with scarlet devotion.

FIRSTS

Bolinao Province,
The Philippine Islands

During monsoon season,
the village lights flicker off
each night around nine o'clock.

Behind bamboo picture frames,
lizards crawl alive and watch
the slight breathing, the coming

together of bodies below.
One woman lies alone, her cheek
seeking a cool fold on her pillow

this thick, wet air won't let her find.
Staring out her single window,
she remembers how they brought

Hector home to her, a hole shot
through his neck: "Ang talaga, Inay."
I'm at peace, Mother. Her eyelids

close, she thinks of firsts:
first words—n*oko eet*, first bread
on his tongue— St. James Church,

his first hunt of wild pigs—how
he was the very product of the first time
she ever opened her legs for a man—

the blood from his mouth bubbled
like iced grapes, popping into wine
down his neck and into her hands—
first, *this.*

4

WORKING THE RICE
Banaue, Philippines

Toes are first to bend
in wrinkles. At the base
of the Panawe Rice Terraces,
I stand flamingo to examine my foot.

My pistachio toes
have had too much water,
too much light climbing these
green steps. My skin smells like

the orange salamanders
dodging our wrinkled hands
as we break the water to pull
the rice roots. I peek at the other *trabajadoras*—

by now their feet
must be tuberous plants
rooted in the slips of earth.
I want to retire to cool, wooden floors,

puffing dust clouds
with each step. I want to eat
chico fruit, sweet lanka, anything
but rice. I want to crush cricket shells

with my heel, hear
their cellophane sound
in death. You devilish vegetable,
push your shoots tomorrow and tomorrow,

but enough for today. Under
my hat, I mutter sunless words:
pagod na pagod—careful so my supervisor
will not hear. My tongue catches a drop of sweat

in the corner of my mouth.
Sometimes these steps ripple
upward on their own, as if we climb past
our very hilltop, high enough to brush young rain, cloud, wing.

OOTY LAKE

"...where it is quite possible to arrange an elephant ride and see
many other wild animals."
—*Guide for Traveling Abroad in India*

The man yells *Audivaggani!* and smacks the beast's back leg. My saddle
is oily and fringed with tassel, all around us a gurgle of magpie, insect,
lake. Black monkeys zip through the elephant's legs as we rumble
ahead and I lean over to shoo them from their game. There sits a tiger
with toes spread into the shoreline, one tooth curling over his lip
like a joke no one forgets. In eighth grade, I asked a boy to dance
who said *I'm not feeling that wild right now* and would I consider
another? Another boy, another song? I did not ask; all night I sipped
cola with Sara and wondered when and where I'd find a wild one
who dances, who sings, who sees all the reds of a jungle.

WRAP

I don't mean when a movie ends,
as in, *It's a*! Nor tortillas splitting
with the heavy wet of bean.
And I don't mean what you do

with your lavender robe—all fluff
and socks—to snatch the paper
from the shrubs. Nor the promise
of a gift, the curl and furl of red ribbon

just begging to be tugged. What I mean
is waiting with my grandmama (a pause
in the Monsoon) at the Trivandrum airport
for a jeep. Her small hand wraps

again the emerald green pallu of her sari
tucked in at her hips, across her breast,
and coughs it up over her shoulder— hush
of paprika and burnt honey across my face.

TABLE MANNERS

In India, Northerners pride themselves
on eating only with their fingertips,
while Southerners enjoy their foods
with the entire hand, to the wrist if need be.

No wonder JoAnn and I sit stunned
at the dinner table as my cousins
scoop and slurp their lunch: dried fish
in gingilly oil, poori soaked first

in sambar then cooled in cucumber rayta.
I motion to Oomana, the servant girl:
do you have fork, spoon? She laughs
a little longer than necessary,

disappears into the storage room.
Each finger-lick makes us grimace
but secretly I want to join them
in slick-smacking this beautiful food.

The three-year old sees my fork
and cries until he gets one
of his own to bang and draw
lines in his plate of sauce.

No one in India ever wishes
you happiness and now I know why:
this is supposed to be of your own doing,
your own relish, from your own open hands.

PEACOCKS

At Chowpatty Beach, people strip
only from the ankles down. Yogis

bury themselves up to the neck
in sand, each turban tagged

with a single blue medallion. I watch
as a little boy offers a violet guava—

the yogi turns away, doesn't blink. Here,
everyone looks only into my eyes; not once

do I catch anyone glance at my bare leg.
My neighbor back in Ohio kept

a peacock tied to her sycamore tree.
By winter, the rope shredded

and the peacock walked the stiff grass
freely, a scarf around its neck.

I wanted to steal a feather
and tape it to my jeans. How

a simple turn of head makes
all the difference. All those eyes.

IN THE POTATOES

Early Scots refused to eat (it was not
mentioned in the Bible); leprosy, blindness—
its supposed price. *"One potato,
two potato, three potato, four!"*
Misunderstood too: Captain Cook,
Walter Raleigh, even Catherine the Great

tried to convince people of the glorious crop
but failed. Lord Byron lamented its aphrodisiac effects:
"...'Tis after all a sad result of passions and potatoes."
The Quencha Indians of Peru have over one thousand
words for this crop. They dance a two-step during harvest,
pant legs rolled to knees, every jump a push of water

from the bitter, marble-sized tubers to make *chuno* paste.
In the blackfrost night, it dries, feeds a whole village
for two seasons: crystal starch. Potato spirits
made of rock line up in threes, hum soil-songs
through rooftops into ears of sleeping infants.
Estar en las papas—to be in the potatoes—

means a person has finally risen to afford more
than a banana diet. In the Paucartambo Valley
of Peru, I read the soft earth like Braille, gather
some on my own—each hardness a possibility.
Tiny pineapples, coral snakes, purple gumdrops,
anything but the brown oval spud I know. A small, flat one—

mishipasinghan—means *cat's nose*; a knobby,
difficult-to-peel one is *lumchipamundana*—or, *potato
makes young bride weep.* The Acumbo village
sees a surplus of the troublesome kind in late summer.
Housewives grind their teeth with each peel,
stifle shivers into aprons, curse the abundant fruit.

WINTER GAMES

On their January honeymoon, Edison and wife experimented with electrocuting oysters. Someone stole all three oranges—pendulant, still tinged green—from my mother's backyard. She made a sign out of an old box flap that said, "WHO STOLE IT?" carefully lettered in black ball-point, tied it with green thread into the branches of her tree. My dog is a blue snowplow in front of me searching for wet unmentionables in plastic bags left over from Fall. I have no idea who stuffed a riot of pine cones and holly in my mailbox. All over the beach hundreds of oysters bubble their last breath, shells blown wide open.

LEWIS AND CLARK DISAGREE

Because Merriwether ate the last berry
without consulting William. Because

that prairie dog only let *William* feed
it dried corn. Because the Nez Perce

gave one and not the other a necklace
of purple quartz. Because osage oranges

gave Merriwether hives. Because a grizzly
chased William into an oak tree, left him

high for hours. Because "Someone" tucked
buffalo chips into Merriwether's knapsack

when he wasn't looking. Because after walking,
rowing, swimming, climbing, trotting, pulling,

cutting, all they really wanted was a name
for a fruit one found sour, the other, so sweet.

SARA, EMBARRASSED

The alpacas were special ordered from Peru.
"Gonna make some sweaters, Hal?"
Neighbors snorted as the noise and the mess
in his backyard grew, but Harold Sutherland
kept thumbing through the latest issue
of *Exotic Animals as Pets!* month after month while
peacocks, ostriches, and an emu arrived at his door.

Across town, prom night:
Stretch limo look what Rachel snuck for the punch satin shoes /
 look at her hair how did it
get so big zip me up I really need a smoke I'm dancing with Billy/
 I don't care if she sees
check out Mr. Wollenberg dance I lost my pin I need more film/
 the room's spinning.

We left the afterparty with bruised corsages
dripping from our wrists and stars canopied
above in the crisp April. In the distance, a strange silhouette
appeared, Sara Sutherland said she forgot something,
ran inside. Her grandfather just smiled and waved—
disappearing over the hill on Taylor Hollow Road,
guiding his llama by the chin-strap.

MIRROR LAKE

You half expect dwarves with little red caps
to appear, but they don't—the plash
of Labradors tossed in by frat-boy owners
probably scares them away. And maybe too,
the eyes of the ducks rolling back
into their handle heads just before
they attack the one that snatches an edge
of bread. My first kiss in college was a guy
who spoke mainly in iambs, but not *here*,
as if I wouldn't somehow remember his speech
was all wrong. And I wonder who collected
snap-violets and left them in tiny piles,
a party pack for squirrels, a tiny offering
of love for men who cannot reach.

FALLING THIRDS

We measure our names the same.
Across the world, when children
call out for a friend, their mother,
their favorite white goat—they have
the same intonation, the same fall
and lilt to their voice, no matter
their language: *Jahhn-ee! Mah-ma!*
Pehh-dro! My music teacher friend
says this is *falling thirds*: this is proof
we spoke the same language before
Babel, that maybe a tower did fall
into rock and dust, gilding our tongues
even slicker past any understanding.
We speak little wants, call little kisses
into our ears across beanfields, sand,
saltwater. Still, we sing the same songs.

CONFUSIONS

Honeybees hum the correct curtsy
to their queen, smudge pollen
in the right waxy cell. Roaches
the size of a baby's sweet shoe
die every day but where exactly
are they disposed of? Do I write his silence,
the pulse and flex in his face as we sit
in his Pontiac, his blue breath wetting
the wheel? Year after year, lacy patterns
of star pull birds back South where I look out
over a veranda, count the crashes of water
and rock. I've noticed he's changed
his handwriting—now it's all squares and shelves
small, burnt cakes on a plate, even his O's

ARACHNE

The sweetest medium
is water. I envy the frog;
her mate holds her firm
in a wet embrace, then
the release—an egg froth
on her back and good-bye.
I cannot imagine a hunger
filled, a calm stretch of nerve.

My legs won't even break
the surface to let me dip
my body in. Perhaps a breeze,
perhaps a dew will come
to envelop me. In the branches
of this gum tree, I sigh. This air
is no good. Who knows
what god I will inhale.

ONE BITE

Miracle fruit changes the tongue. One bite,
and for hours all you eat is sweet. Placed
alone on a saucer, it quivers like it's cold
from the ceramic, even in this Florida heat.

Small as a coffee bean, red as jam—
I can't believe. The man who sold
it to my father on Interstate 542 had one
tooth, one sandal, and called me

"Duttah, Duttah." I wanted to ask what
is that, but the red buds teased me
into our car and away from his fruit stand.
One bite. And if you eat it whole, it softens

and swells your teeth like a mouthful
of mallow. So how long before you lose
a sandal and still walk? How long
before you lose the sweetness?

COCOA BEACH, OFF-SEASON

Where sanderlings race to pluck
coquina clams from the sand,
jelly tongues still slapping for wet air.
A place where tourist-trap signs pluralize
things that shouldn't be: *hand-dipped ice creams,*
fantastic surfs. A family umbrellas a picnic
of egg salad sandwiches, canned cola
wrapped in foil, a bag of cherries—
and no one with gaudy gold bangles
or hat brims wide as a pelican's wing
will ever ask them to move please,
you're blocking my sun. Two sisters
pack together sand and foam to make
igloos around their feet. A father jumps
the waves or talks to the local shellbacks
about what they have and haven't caught.
If you're lucky, you'll spy a ghost crab—
how he stands on claw tips, kicking
at his own door in the sand, how he cuts
the sand sideways to a tossed piece of bread.
Best of all are the small impressions
of a mother's feet into a shoreline
soft and dark as unfrosted cake. The prints
say, *Here* is where she lingered over
a Queen Conch shell. Here is where
she stayed the morning to gather bits:
fire sponges, jingle shells, a remnant of whelk.

GOOD BLOOD

You have good blood, the nurse
informs me. Not too thin, and lots
of waxy fat cells, my very own
holly berries decking my veins.
Or does she mean my blood is warm—
not like the Atlantic at the end
of the year, cooling like soup

whenever a storm brews
the other side of the Earth?
Quite possibly, she means
it's the *color* that's just fine—
not purple, the pox
on my mother's plum tree—
not brown like weevils burying

themselves into acorns
on my street—but red, as in
pepper, wine, finch throats,
a ladybeetle's shell, the star
my father always points out
to me on my birthday,
two days before His.

SPEAK

If the Hopi say "ripi"
to mean *notch*, then
for them, *serration*
is "ripiripiripi." I want
to speak like that, fill
your ears and hands
with wet stones, turquoise
and smooth, as if
they had tumbled
in the mouth of a macaw.

WHAT I LEARNED FROM THE INCREDIBLE HULK

When it comes to clothes, make
an allowance for the unexpected.
Be sure the spare in the trunk
of your station wagon with wood paneling

isn't in need of repair. A simple jean jacket
says *Hey, if you aren't trying to smuggle*
rare Incan coins through this peaceful
little town and kidnap the local orphan,

I can be one heck of a mellow kinda guy.
Green doesn't always mean envy.
It's the wide meadows full of clover
and chicory that the Hulk seeks

for rest, a return to normal. Sometimes,
a woman gets to go with him, her tiny hands
correcting his rumpled hair, the cuts
in his hand. And no matter how angry

a man gets, a smile and a soft stroke
on his bicep can work wonders.
I learned that male chests *also*
have nipples, warm and established—

that I'd be attracted to loners, all
their valuables in one bag in case
they had to leave and quick—and oh,
how I love to get in their way.

OUR TIME

So this is what's become of us:
feed dog, water dog, walk dog.
Even my most excellent clothes
are sprinkled with dog hair.
We've become a cartoon,
the people we always made fun of,
putting dogs in sweaters and vinyl booties.
Our time is the pretzel of our legs,
tracing the outline of your lips
on my neck after you've fallen
asleep. It's setting our clock
ten minutes after you wake, so when
you are in the middle of shaving,
patting your face, I can rise
from our bed, sneak down the hallway,
into the bathroom, and pull off
the towel wrapped at your waist.

SPICES

coloring
If your man doesn't know cumin
from cardamom, it's time to let him go.
But if he discovers a wetted paintbrush dipped
into turmeric makes a soft yellow line
on your back, spells something like *You
are my sun*—then keep him girl, and hold on tight.
I like a cupboard packed with jam jars rubbed clean,
full of the sand from fantasy beaches of me
and my man and a paintbrush I conjured up
just last night—a cupboard where the difference in reds
means danger or victory for my pot of stew.

fragrance
And what about cloves pierced
into a fat orange, strung up with ribbon
at Christmas? Who came up with that,
and what kind of twisted need did they have
for the occasional prick of spikes under
nails? Once, when we were leaving
Bombay Palace, my father spooned
caraway and licorice bits into my palm
from the jade bowl on the counter and said,
"This will clean your breath." The owner
twitched his mustache, and nodded.

heat
Pepper is the obvious choice, in its powder form,
I mean--but there's something about the crush
of peppercorns into a salad, over pasta, the twist
and flex of wrist that sends men back for more.
But if you really want to impress, try chili flaked fresh
under a rolling pin and wax paper. Make sure he sees
you doing this labor of love—act as if you do this
at every meal, that this is how it would be every day
if he desired. And after dinner, float some
in his tea, slip some into his slice of cake.
Be careful for the warmth of his mouth.

LATE

He is too late for knives
and cutting boards wet with the juice
of fresh salmon, or maybe perch—
no time for cilantro to stick

under his nails. When he greets her *hello*
with his hand to her cheek, she'll know
exactly what will be on her plate. If he
didn't have to walk the dog, he'd be slicing

butter into a hot pan, striping cucumbers
and Walla Walla onions into a salad.
Instead, he pulls a thin box
from the freezer, zips a slice of air

into the apple crisp, the butterbar squash,
the meatloaf. The dial is set for five
and he steps away from the huzz
of the oven to check the street below.

He's late and he knows how she hates
to dash from car to theater, how
she'll lean away from him in the dark,
how he still needs time to buy his popcorn:

salt, no oil. The skin just under his earlobe
sweats lightly as he eats—skin that she likes
to tap with a finger, skin thin as a piece
of fresh vellum, just ripe for a calligraphy.

MOUTH STORIES

"Its ridges, valleys, the corrugated roof, the fortress of teeth.
There's a story trapped inside my mouth."
— Jeanette Winterson's *Written on the Body*

sweet

Tight places between the molars,
the hollow under the tongue—
syrup-thick with desire, I find
my favorite place on your chest,
your lips parted small while you sleep,
banana ice cream kiss.

sour

I leave your house before you
wake. The smash-smash of dead
leaves crumbles from the dark
corners of your frown. The ink
on yesterday's paper, cover
from the rain, drools down my cheek.

bitter

Like unripened pears for breakfast,
I taste a green skin in the back of my throat
when I think of your breath
warming someone else's thigh—
bottom lip cracked cold, I swallow
the last bit of blood.

salty

The skin between your shoulder
and neck is fresh on my tongue.
The first tear from your Bohemian
blue eye I lapped up by chance,
the second on purpose; I cannot rid
this taste from my mouth.

Colophon

Fishbone was set in a computer version of Caslon. The original Caslon typeface was cut by the English typefounder William Caslon and was first shown in his specimen of 1734; it was recut by the Monotype Corporation in 1915. The book was printed by Courier Printing of Deposit, New York.

Other Poetry Titles from the Snail's Pace Press, Inc.

Field Guide to the Ineffable: Poems on Marcel Duchamp
by Grace Bauer.

These highly original, intelligent poems based on the life and work of French surrealist Marcel Duchamp are frequently surprising and humorous. The poems evoke not only the spirit of Duchamp, but the best of contemporary American poetry. Grace Bauer's previous collections include *The Women at The Well* (Portals Press), *Where You've Seen Her* (Pennywhistle Press) and *The House Where I've Never Lived* (Anabiosis Press). She has been awarded an Academy of American Poets' Prize, an Irene Leache Poetry Prize and an Individual Artist's Fellowship from the Virginia Commission for the Arts. Ms. Bauer teaches creative writing at the University of Nebraska in Lincoln.
    32 pages, perfect bound $6.00/$7.00 post-paid

Green Tombs to Jupiter by Barry Ballard

Barry Ballard's collection of lyrical blank verse sonnets inhabit contemporary settings and tell stories with precise imagery and metaphor. His poems have appeared in *American Literary Review, Midwestern Quarterly, Paris/Atlantic*, and *Barbaric Yawp*, among many others. He has gained national attention for his poetry, including an Award for Literature from the University of Alaska in 1999. Barry Ballard was born in rural Holt, Michigan. After returning from Vietnam, he earned an M.A. in theology and philosophy from Texas Christian University. *Green Tombs to Jupiter* is his first published collection.
    32 pages, perfect bound $6.00/$7.00 post-paid

Order from:

The Snail's Pace Press, Inc.
85 Darwin Road
Cambridge, New York 12816
snail@poetic.com